Jerry Rice

Additional Titles in the Sports Reports Series

Andre Agassi
Star Tennis Player
(0-89490-798-0)

Troy Aikman
Star Quarterback
(0-89490-927-4)

Charles Barkley
Star Forward
(0-89490-655-0)

Ken Griffey, Jr.
Star Outfielder
(0-89490-802-2)

Wayne Gretzky
Star Center
(0-89490-930-4)

Michael Jordan
Star Guard
(0-89490-482-5)

Jim Kelly
Star Quarterback
(0-89490-446-9)

Shawn Kemp
Star Forward
(0-89490-929-0)

Mario Lemieux
Star Center
(0-89490-932-0)

Karl Malone
Star Forward
(0-89490-931-2)

Dan Marino
Star Quarterback
(0-89490-933-9)

Mark Messier
Star Center
(0-89490-801-4)

Chris Mullin
Star Forward
(0-89490-486-8)

Hakeem Olajuwon
Star Center
(0-89490-803-0)

Shaquille O'Neal
Star Center
(0-89490-656-9)

Jerry Rice
Star Wide Receiver
(0-89490-928-2)

Cal Ripken Jr.
Star Shortstop
(0-89490-485-X)

David Robinson
Star Center
(0-89490-483-3)

Barry Sanders
Star Running Back
(0-89490-484-1)

Deion Sanders
Star Athlete
(0-89490-652-6)

Junior Seau
Star Linebacker
(0-89490-800-6)

Emmitt Smith
Star Running Back
(0-89490-653-4)

Frank Thomas
Star First Baseman
(0-89490-659-3)

Thurman Thomas
Star Running Back
(0-89490-445-0)

Chris Webber
Star Forward
(0-89490-799-9)

Steve Young
Star Quarterback
(0-89490-654-2)

Jerry Rice

Star Wide Receiver

Stew Thornley

Enslow Publishers, Inc.

44 Fadem Road	PO Box 38
Box 699	Aldershot
Springfield, NJ 07081	Hants GU12 6BP
USA	UK

Library of Congress Cataloging-in-Publication Data

Thornley, Stew.
     Jerry Rice: star wide receiver / Stew Thornley.
        p. cm.—(Sports reports)
     Includes bibliographical references (p.) and index.
     Summary: Profiles the personal life and professional career
of the record setting receiver of the San Francisco 49ers.
     ISBN 0-89490-928-2
     1. Rice, Jerry—Juvenile literature. 2. Football players—United States—
Biography—Juvenile literature. 3. San Francisco 49ers (Football team)—Juvenile
literature. [1. Rice, Jerry. 2. Football players. 3. Afro-Americans—Biography.
4. San Francisco 49ers (Football team)] I. Title. II. Series.
GV939.R53T56   1998
796.332'092
[B]—DC21   97-20379
                                              CIP
                                              AC

Printed in the United States of America

10 9 8 7 6 5 4 3 2

Photo Credits: © 1993 Mickey Pfleger, p. 79; © 1994 Mickey Pfleger, p. 9;
© 1995 Mickey Pfleger, Sports California, pp. 13, 18, 20; © Mickey Pfleger,
pp. 25, 29, 37, 48, 84; Minnesota Vikings, p. 58; San Francisco 49ers, pp. 40,
65, 68, 69, 72, 76, 89; © Scott Cunningham, p. 90.

Cover Photo: © 1995 Mickey Pfleger, Sports California.

Contents

Chapter 1

Catching a Legend

The opening game of the 1994 National Football League (NFL) season was an important one for the San Francisco 49ers. After a couple of years of disappointing playoff losses, the team was determined to get back to the Super Bowl. A good start to the season would be a big step in that direction. The first game, against the Los Angeles Raiders, would be played on a Monday night for a national television audience. For many viewers, though, the focus of this game would not be on the 49ers as a team but on one of their players. Jerry Rice, San Francisco's great receiver, was on the verge of making history.

Few people had expected such greatness from Rice when he entered the league nine years before.

Coming out of a small college in Mississippi, Rice was overlooked by many pro teams. Some coaches thought Rice did not have the breakaway speed he needed to be a star in the NFL. Rice got a chance with the San Francisco 49ers, however, and he proved the experts wrong. The road to being No. 1 was paved with hard work for Rice. He combined his talent with a work ethic that became legendary around the league. The off-season workouts he participated in were known for their intensity.

Rice also showed himself to be a durable—and fearless—type of player. Many receivers make their living running sideline patterns. They catch a pass and get out of bounds before being tackled. Rice's trademark is a slant pattern that takes him out into the middle of the field. He often finds himself in a den of angry linebackers who love to dish out punishment. Some receivers shy away from this kind of contact. Rice, on the other hand, thoroughly enjoys it. "I like the contact, and I like the courage, being able to go in there, knowing you're going to get hit, and still catch the football."[1]

Rice can take the hard hits when they come his way. "It's a challenge to see if you can get across the middle and still come out in one piece," he says.[2] But often, the defensive team never gets the chance to lay a hand on him.

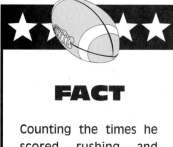

FACT

Counting the times he scored rushing and receiving, Rice reached 100 touchdowns for his career in October 1992. Only seven other players had reached that level before. They are:

Jim Brown	126
Walter Payton	125
John Riggins	116
Lenny Moore	113
Don Hutson	105
Steve Largent	101
Franco Harris	100

Jerry Rice catches another pass, one of many in an outstanding career as a wide reciever for the San Francisco 49ers.

What puts Rice in a class of his own is what he can do after he catches the ball. "I feel like the fun is just starting after I catch the football," Rice has said.[3] Many times in his career, Rice has turned a short pass into a big gain. Some receivers search for the safety of the sidelines after making a catch. Rice, on the other hand, seeks refuge in the opposition's end zone.

Through his first nine seasons in the NFL, Rice had reached the end zone 124 times. Only two players—Walter Payton of the Chicago Bears and Jim Brown of the Cleveland Browns—had ever scored more touchdowns. Both of these players were running backs, who got many more chances to touch the ball—and score touchdowns—than pass catchers like Rice did. Rice already held the NFL record for receiving touchdowns.

Now, coming into the 1994 season, he was within striking distance of the record for touchdowns of any type. One would tie him with Payton; two would put him into a tie with Brown for the top spot. If he could cross the goal line three times, he would be the all-time touchdown leader.

Rice was more concerned with the success of his team than with personal glory. However, he knew the best way to get the spotlight off of him and back on the 49ers would be to break the record as soon as he could. Steve Young, the 49ers star quarterback, felt the same way. He would try to pass the ball to Rice as much as possible.

Passing the ball would be treacherous this evening, however. Strong winds whipped in all directions at San Francisco's Candlestick Park while fog rolled in off the nearby bay. But it would take more than wind and fog to stop this tandem. They decided to strike early. In scouting the Raiders during preseason games, the San Francisco coaches had noticed that Raider defensive backs could be fooled on run fakes. The safeties would hold their ground when they thought one of the running backs was taking a hand-off. That moment of hesitation could be costly when the play turned out to be a pass, especially when Jerry Rice was the receiver heading downfield. An opposing cornerback had once said, covering Rice is "like a horror show. He's so smooth when he's running. He gets right on top of you and before you know it, he's by you. Once he is, I don't think anybody's going to catch him."[4]

The Raider defenders had to agree with this assessment the first time the 49ers had the ball. Young knew they had the chance for a big play if he could get the Los Angeles defensive backs to bite. After taking the snap at his own 31-yard line, Young faked a hand-off, kept the ball, and looked downfield. Rice had taken off and was already behind the secondary.

Young heaved a long pass. At full stride, Rice caught the ball at the Los Angeles 30-yard line and kept on running. Cornerback Lionel Washington dived at Rice. He managed to get a hand on him. This caused Rice to stumble, but he regained his balance and continued on for a 69-yard touchdown.

The fans went wild and hoped for more. The 49ers continued to build their lead into the second half; however, other players, not Rice, did the scoring. Early in the fourth quarter, though, the 49ers fooled the Raiders in a different way. Young handed off to Ricky Watters, who in turn handed the ball to Rice, who was coming from the opposite way. The play was a reverse, designed to trap the defense into moving in the wrong direction. The play worked beautifully and turned into a 23-yard touchdown run for Rice. He had now tied Brown at the top of the all-time touchdown list.

Rice did not think he would get the record to himself in this game. With just over four minutes left, the 49ers were leading the Raiders, 37–14. When a team is that far ahead with so little time left, it will usually take its star players out of the game, so they will not be injured in a game that the team is sure to win.

Rice figured that would be the case as he picked

Jerry Rice lifts his arms in celebration after tying Jim Brown's record for the most touchdowns scored in NFL history.

up a sideline phone connected to offensive coordinator Mike Shanahan in the press box. Rice expected that Shanahan would congratulate him on tying Brown and would tell him to take a seat on the bench. Instead, Shanahan told Rice he would get one more shot at the record as the 49ers took over the ball on the Raiders' 38-yard line.

Rice and Young trotted back out with the rest of the offensive squad. On the first play, Rice went in motion behind the line of scrimmage and took off on a post pattern when the ball was snapped. Cornerback Albert Lewis did a good job of staying with Rice. Back behind the line, Young was under pressure. He backpedaled and released a pass just before being leveled by defensive end Scott Davis. The pass was underthrown, but Rice adjusted. He cut in front of Lewis, jumped high into the air, grabbed the ball at the 2-yard line, and held on as he fell into the end zone.

Rice had done it. His third touchdown of the game also made him the top touchdown scorer in the history of the NFL. "I'm really so happy to get it done," he said after the game. "When I caught that last ball, so much pressure left my body. I was so emotional."[5]

Chapter 2

Building a Strong Foundation

If I wasn't playing football, I'd be doing something with my hands—electronics, or maybe something with cars. It doesn't matter. I've always liked working with my hands."[1] Indeed, as a young man Jerry Rice had learned to fix anything with his hands. He felt this would be his ticket out of the isolated area of Mississippi where he grew up.

Jerry Rice was one of the eight children of Joe and Eddie B. Rice. He was the sixth child born. He has one older sister, four older brothers, a younger brother, and a younger sister. The family lived outside of Crawford, Mississippi, a town of about five hundred people. One writer characterized this part of Mississippi as a place with "... no street lights, sidewalks, traffic signs—no drugs or crime."[2]

Crawford was so small that its library was housed in a forty-foot house trailer that also served as the town's civic center.

Crawford, Mississippi, is in Oktibbeha County. Around the county is a great deal of brickwork that is the work of Jerry's father. Joe Rice was a brick mason who also put his sons to work in the business. "One of my brothers would stack about four bricks on top of one each other and toss them up," Rice explained. "They might go this way and that way, and I would catch all four. "I did it so many times, it was just a reaction."[3] "Catching bricks taught me the meaning of hard work."[4]

Jerry also started to develop his running ability. Sometimes he and his brothers would go into a neighbor's field. If they could catch the horses in the field, they could ride them. It took a great deal of quickness to grab one of the horses. "They didn't just come to you," Rice pointed out. "If you wanted to ride, you chased them down."[5] Later, when Jerry Rice played sports in high school, the only way to get home after practice was on foot. The five-mile jogs on the dirt roads leading out of Crawford gave him added strength and stamina.

When Jerry Rice was thirteen years old, he watched Lynn Swann play in Super Bowl X for the Pittsburgh Steelers. Rice was a big fan of Swann's and he was thrilled when Swann was named Most Valuable Player of that game. Lynn Swann was the first receiver ever to receive that honor. Despite this, Rice was not thinking about following in his hero's footsteps. Jerry Rice was busy using his athletic talents in other sports—as a forward in basketball and a high jumper in track and field.

In addition to being a good athlete, Jerry Rice was a good student. He was more interested in his studies than in sports. But it was, in fact, a brief lapse from schoolwork that got him into football. During his sophomore year, he played hooky from school. He was skipping a class when the vice principal spotted him and called out his name. Jerry took off running. The vice principal was not happy with him for cutting class or for running away, but he was impressed with the young man's speed. He offered to let up on the punishment if Jerry would report to Charles Davis, the football coach at B. L. Moor High School. The football team could use an athlete like Jerry Rice. After getting a good look at him, Davis agreed.

One person who was not happy about the situation was Jerry's mom. She objected to his playing such a violent sport. "I didn't love it," she said about her son's playing football. "But the more I fought it, the more determined he was, so I gave it

Keeping his eyes on the ball, Jerry Rice grabs another pass. Rice began to develop his catching abilities while working with his father as a young boy.

up."[6] Tom Rice, Jerry's older brother, was already playing college football at Jackson State University. Their mother had to get used to the idea of watching them play this sport.

Jerry Rice played several positions on the football team, on both offense and defense. It was at wide receiver that he excelled, however. He was an immediate sensation at that position, and he got better every year.

B. L. Moor was a small school. It had barely five hundred students spread out over twelve grade levels. As a result, few fans attended the school's football games. The team also got little coverage in newspapers around the state, even though it was winning most of its games.

The quarterback for B.L. Moor High School was Willie Gillespie. Rice and Gillespie spent a great deal of time together, practicing. They did not just get together at organized team practices, either. The two worked out on their own time, perfecting their timing and their game. Rice and Gillespie had a chemistry between them. It was something that Rice would develop with other quarterbacks with whom he played in college and in the NFL.

Jerry Rice had a spectacular senior season. He caught 80 passes and scored 35 touchdowns. Usually, such a performance would get a player all

Jerry Rice looks to make a move on an approaching defender. Rice used to chase horses when he was young. This may have helped to develop his quickness on the field.

sorts of offers for college scholarships. That was not the case with Rice, though. It seemed that no one had noticed how good he was. Even Mississippi State University, located only twenty miles from Crawford, did not send anyone to watch him play.

Jackson State University heard about Jerry Rice from his brother Tom, but Jackson State's offense was built around a running game. Coach W. C. Gordon was not interested in a receiver like Jerry Rice.

Fortunately, there was one school that knew it could use a player like Jerry Rice. Mississippi Valley State was a predominantly African-American school located in tiny Itta Bena, seventy-five miles west of Crawford. Founded in 1950 on a former cotton patch, the school had just 2,580 students. Mississippi Valley State was not one of the big college football powerhouses. It would give Rice a chance to show his stuff, however. At this point, that was all he was asking for.

FACT

Following his rookie season in the NFL, Rice built a new home for his parents in Starkville, Mississippi. This had been a long-time dream for Rice and his brother Tom. Tom played college football at Jackson State but was not drafted by a professional team.

Chapter 3

A Daring Delta Devil

Jerry Rice was not going to college just to play football. He fully intended to get an education while he was at Mississippi Valley State. He chose electronics as his major—still focusing on his ability to fix things.

While Rice studied electronics in the classroom, outside, on the football field he was also electrifying. His coach, Archie Cooley, said there was really nothing about Rice's size or speed that made him stand out from others. "But he had those hands," said Cooley, "and he had that desire to improve."[1]

Cooley had been an All-American center and linebacker when he played football for Jackson State in the late 1950s and early 1960s. Cooley was in only his second year of coaching the Mississippi Valley

State Delta Devils when Jerry Rice joined the team in 1981. Cooley, however, was already well known for his colorful style. He wore a black cowboy hat on the sideline during games and was known by the nickname "Gunslinger." The name came from Cooley's style and his ability to pass the ball.

Under Cooley, the Delta Devils put on a great offensive show. They would often have five receivers going out for a pass on a given play. When Jerry Rice came to the team, Cooley changed the offense to make it even more exciting. He devised interesting and bizarre plays designed to spring Rice loose.

The Delta Devils played in the Southwestern Athletic Conference (SWAC). All of the schools with teams in the conference were considered Division I–AA schools by the National Collegiate Athletic Association (NCAA). This is one step below the big schools that are in Division I–A. Being in the lower division meant little national exposure for the players and teams. This had its drawbacks, but it also had its advantages, as Rice pointed out:

> Going to Mississippi Valley State was a blessing. If I had gone to a major school, I don't think I would have been able to make as much progress in both academics and football. I was a shy kid coming out of high school. I might have been swallowed up by a big-time university.[2]

Rice's great hands set him apart from other receivers. It is very rare to see him drop a pass.

Rice already knew the meaning of hard work before he got to college. But with Coach Cooley constantly pushing him, Rice cemented the work ethic that he carried with him throughout his NFL career.

Gloster Richardson was the receivers' coach for the Delta Devils. He had been a great receiver in both the American and National Football Leagues and had played on Super Bowl championship teams with the Kansas City Chiefs and Dallas Cowboys. Richardson noticed other qualities that made Rice so good. "He has developed such concentration and field sense, and his routes are so precise. Plus he comes across the field with so much intensity, guys seem like they are getting out of his way."[3]

Rice had a good freshman year, with 30 receptions. He more than doubled that total in 1982, catching 66 passes as a sophomore. By this time, the Delta Devils had a new quarterback, Willie "Satellite" Totten. Totten got his nickname because he was so accurate with his passes. It was said he could beam the ball into a receiver's hands. When those hands were as good as Rice's, it made for a great combination.

Totten and his receivers were a close-knit bunch. They would arrive at practice an hour earlier than the rest of the team so that they could work on pass patterns together. Totten and Rice were especially close. It was not long before Rice acquired a colorful nickname of his own—much like Totten had done. Outstanding players often win awards known as "All-Conference" or "All-America." Jerry Rice was so good that people said he was "All-World." From that came his nickname, "World."

Opposing teams knew how good Rice was. They often put two defenders on him. When that did not work, they went to three defenders, but Rice still found a way to make catches. Once, against Jackson State, Rice was being triple-teamed. Totten was being chased behind the line of scrimmage. He could not find an open receiver, so he just heaved a pass downfield. He figured it would sail over the end zone, and at least he would not be tackled for a loss. To Totten's surprise, it turned into a touchdown completion when Rice jumped high in the end zone to pluck the pass out of the air.

Rice beat his defenders with his leaping ability on that play. Often, he would shake some of his defenders loose with a series of smooth cuts. He had a simple formula for beating a triple-team: "You've got to get rid of the first man, run the pattern on the second man and take the ball away from the third man."[4]

Rice made many great catches on the football

field. He also made a great catch off it. He met his wife, Jackie, while he was at Mississippi Valley State. She was studying medicine at the University of Southern Mississippi at Hattiesburg, on the other side of the state. One weekend, Jackie visited friends at Itta Bena. They took her to one of the Delta Devils' basketball games, and Rice was also at the game. Jackie did not know that he was a big star on the school's football team. The two hit it off, stayed in touch, and eventually got married.

By 1983 the Satellite Express offense was in full gear. The Delta Devils won their first two games by big margins. They beat Morris Brown, 49–7, in the season opener, then demolished Arkansas-Pine Bluff, 63–0. Two weeks later, Mississippi Valley State hosted Southern University, and Rice went wild. He caught 24 passes for 279 yards to set new Division I–AA records in both categories. The feats were overshadowed by a couple of things, though. One was that one of the officials, Ralph Willis, suffered a fatal heart attack during the game. The other was that the Delta Devils lost the game.

Crowds continued to pack Magnolia Stadium in Itta Bena to watch the Delta Devils. They beat Texas Southern University in their homecoming game as Totten and Rice hooked up on a 71-yard touchdown pass. The following week, at Prairie View A & M,

Jerry Rice enjoys spending quality time with his wife, Jackie, and daughter Jaqui. Jerry and Jackie met while he was a student at Mississippi Valley State.

Totten threw for 7 touchdowns. Three were to Rice, who ended up with 242 yards receiving.

After the loss to Southern University, Mississippi Valley State went undefeated the rest of the year. They tied Grambling State and won their other five games to finish the year with a record of 7 wins, 2 losses, and one tie.

Rice ended up with 102 catches in 1983. He would do even better his senior season. The Delta Devils opened the 1984 season with a nonconference game at Kentucky State. They won by a score of 86–0 as Totten threw for 9 scoring passes. Rice caught 5 of the touchdowns. He also had 294 yards in receiving, to break the record he had set the year before.

The Totten-Rice combination stayed hot. Through the team's first four games, Totten had thrown 27 touchdown passes. Rice had 64 catches for 917 yards and 12 touchdowns during that span. In addition to the blowout over Kentucky State, the Delta Devils beat Washburn, 77–15; Jackson State, 49–32; and Southern University, 63–45. In the win over Southern, Rice not only scored twice, but threw 2 touchdown passes.

After beating Grambling State, 48–36, for its fifth win of the year, Mississippi Valley State was ranked No. 1 in the Sheridan Broadcasting Network Poll of African-American college football teams. Even so, most people paid little attention to the outstanding season the Delta Devils were having. Rice was terrific, but his exploits were being overlooked. But one NFL coach did get the opportunity, almost by accident, to see how good Rice was.

Mississippi Valley State's sixth game of the 1984 season was at Southern University in Houston. By chance, the San Francisco 49ers were also in town to play the Houston Oilers the next day. Bill Walsh, the 49ers' coach, was too tense the night before the game to sleep well. He turned on the television set to catch some sports news. The Houston station Walsh watched showed highlights of the Delta Devils' 55–42 win. The highlights included two long touchdown receptions by Rice.

Walsh was impressed with what he saw of Rice. He sent one of the team's scouts, Tommy Hart, to Itta Bena to check Rice out in person the following week. Hart was just as impressed as he watched Rice score 5 touchdowns.

Mississippi Valley State had a 5–0 record in conference play at the end of October. Their next game was against the Alcorn State Braves, the only other undefeated team in the SWAC. The Braves won this game. It would be the Delta Devils' only loss of the regular season. Rice ended up breaking his own record by catching 103 passes in 1984. He

STATS

Jerry Rice held eighteen Division I-AA records when he finished his college career at Mississippi Valley State. They included:

24 receptions in a game against Southern University in 1983
103 receptions in a season, 1984
301 receptions in a career
294 receiving yards in a game against Kentucky State in 1984
1,682 receiving yards in a season, 1984
4,693 receiving yards in a career
23 games in a career with at least 100 receiving yards in a game
26 games in a career with a touchdown catch
5 touchdown receptions in a game against Kentucky State and Prairie View
   A & M, 1984
27 touchdown receptions in a season, 1984
50 touchdown receptions in a career

set other records, with 28 touchdown receptions for the season and 50 for his college career.

Even though Mississippi Valley State did not win the conference championship, the team did advance to the Division I–AA playoffs. However, it was eliminated quickly with a 66–19 loss to Louisiana Tech. It was a disappointing finish to a great year for Mississippi Valley State, but for Rice, the season was not over yet. He was selected to play for the Gray team in the Blue-Gray Classic on Christmas Day in 1984. The Gray team clung to a 7–6 lead in the second quarter when Kurt Page, a quarterback from Vanderbilt, hit Rice with a 14-yard touchdown pass. The play gave Gray a 14–6 lead at halftime.

Gray had increased its lead to 20–6 in the fourth quarter. It had the ball on its own 40-yard line, when the quarterback handed off to Paul Ott Carruth. It looked like a running play, but Carruth passed the ball to Rice, who then outraced defenders down the sideline for a 60-yard touchdown. With 4 catches for 101 yards and 2 touchdowns, Rice was named the Most Valuable Player of the Blue-Gray Classic.

Chapter 4

A Rocky Rookie Year

In spring 1985 NFL teams were preparing for the college draft. They were looking at the top college stars from around the country and thinking about which players they would like to have. Few teams were thinking about Jerry Rice, however. Most scouts said he was not fast enough. They said the only reason he had great statistics was because he played against other small schools. One person who was happy to hear this was Bill Walsh, the San Francisco coach, who wanted Rice for the 49ers.

Walsh was considered a great judge of athletic talent. He remembered watching sports highlights of Rice on television in Houston the previous October. Gunslinger Cooley had also sent the 49ers reels of film showing Rice in action. Like others,

Walsh had questions about Rice's speed, but he was impressed with his ability to get into the end zone.

However, one other team, the Dallas Cowboys, did have an eye on Rice. Rice had grown up as a fan of the Cowboys and no doubt would have enjoyed playing for them. Bill Walsh was not going to let that happen, however, even though Dallas would be picking ahead of the 49ers in the draft. The 49ers had just won the Super Bowl. As the team with the best record in the NFL, they had the last pick in the draft. Dallas had the seventeenth selection. But Walsh pulled off a trade with the New England Patriots, who had the sixteenth selection. Walsh got the Patriots' draft spot in the trade. He used it to draft Rice, snatching him away right before the Cowboys could have taken him

Rice finally signed a five-year contract worth $1.8 million on Tuesday, July 23, 1985. He then reported to training camp at Sierra College in Rocklin, California. Rice raised a few eyebrows as he drove up in an expensive car with license plates that spelled W-O-R-L-D, his college nickname.

Rice's style indicated confidence, and so did his words. "All I've really got to do," he said, "is just catch the football and read defenses."[1] Reading the defense—how its lined up, the type of formation its in—can give an offensive player an edge. Rice had

Rice has had many nicknames during his career. One of them "Flash 80" refers to his flashy style off the field, and high uniform number on the field.

been taught how to read defenses by Gunslinger Cooley at Mississippi Valley State. He felt that he would have no trouble doing the same in the NFL.

As for catching the football, he knew that would be a snap. For now, he could see nothing but smooth sailing. "Now it's all in the bag. Routine."[2] As it turned out, though, catching would be a big problem for him during his rookie season.

The 49ers had eleven wide receivers in camp. Walsh planned on keeping only five. Still, Rice was not worried. The coach had made it clear that he would be one of the receivers making the team. Walsh had also said that Rice would challenge veteran Freddie Solomon for a spot in the starting lineup. Although he was ten years older than Rice, Solomon was still an outstanding receiver.

Rice would end up taking the starting spot before the season was over, but Solomon was not bitter. In fact, he did what he could to help Rice. Along with another veteran receiver, Dwight Clark, Solomon helped Rice keep his spirits up during some of the tough times he went through.

In 1984, San Francisco was nearly unbeatable. The 49ers lost only one game all season and cruised to a Super Bowl championship. It was the team's second title in four years. Joe Montana was the quarterback for both championships. By the time Rice

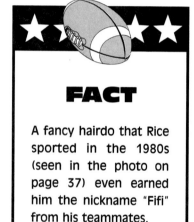

FACT

A fancy hairdo that Rice sported in the 1980s (seen in the photo on page 37) even earned him the nickname "Fifi" from his teammates.

joined the team, Montana was being recognized as one of the best quarterbacks of all time. Eventually, Rice's name would be linked closely with Montana's. The two would hook up on many pass completions and many touchdowns. In the beginning, though, it was a different quarterback who would make his mark with Rice.

Matt Cavanaugh was Montana's backup in 1985. Normally, Cavanaugh would get a chance to play only when Montana was injured, or late in a game in which the 49ers were winning big. In the pre-season, though, coaches try to give all of their players a chance to play.

The 49ers first exhibition game of 1985 was in Los Angeles against the Raiders. Montana played during the first quarter, then Cavanaugh came in. With just six minutes left in the first half, Jerry Rice made the first catch of his professional career. It was a 19-yard strike from Cavanaugh. On the next play, Cavanaugh was knocked out of the game on a hard hit by Raider defensive end Lyle Alzado.

Joe Montana returned and had a chance to connect with Jerry Rice in the end zone. With only seconds left in the half, the Raider line rushed the quarterback. Montana was forced out of the pocket. Scrambling to avoid being tackled, Montana did not see Rice standing alone in the end zone. Instead,

When Jerry Rice joined the San Francisco 49ers, Joe Montana (shown here) was the starting quarterback. During his career, Montana led San Francisco to four Super Bowl championships.

Montana hit tight end John Frank for the score. Rice did not get his first NFL touchdown that day, but he was one of the first players to come over and congratulate John Frank.

Jerry Rice finished his first game in the NFL with 3 catches for 66 yards. He had one, even more memorable catch, but it did not count. Montana hit Rice, running down the right sideline on a play that covered 66 yards. The officials ruled that Rice had stepped out of bounds before making the catch, however. This is against NFL rules, and the catch was wiped out. Montana was dissapointed that the play did not count. He later commented, however, on how impressed he was with Rice's ability.

Rice had a big play that stayed on the books two weeks later. Cavanaugh started at quarterback in the exhibition game against the San Diego Chargers. On the third play of the game, he decided to try for a big play with his rookie receiver. Jerry Rice raced past defensive back Danny Walters on a deep route. Cavanaugh's pass was short, but Rice was able to adjust. He caught the ball at the 10-yard line, and ran the ball in for the touchdown. He finally scored his first touchdown in the NFL.

During training camp and pre-season games, Jerry Rice was impressing the people around him. George Seifert, who later became the head coach of the 49ers, was the defensive coordinator for San Francisco when Rice joined the team. Seifert recalls, "The first training camp I remember distinctly how he intimidated many of our defensive backs to a point where they started off the season without any confidence."[3]

FACT

When Jerry Rice came into the NFL, he was shy and not sure what to say to reporters. After the 1986 season he took speech lessons. This helped him during interviews, and he looks forward to a possible broadcasting career after his playing career is over.

Rice was full of confidence when the regular season opened. The 49ers' first game was at Minnesota, against the Vikings. Rice was not in the starting line-up, but he got a chance to play and did well. Actually, he did better than most of his teammates.

The 49ers were heavy favorites to beat the Vikings, who had won only three games the season before. However, San Francisco hurt itself with fumbles, interceptions, and penalties. They lost possession of the ball seven times because of either a fumble or an interception. Minnesota, an eleven-point underdog coming into the game, scored 2 late touchdowns to win, 28–21. In the game, though, Rice caught all four passes thrown to him. He held on to one even though he was hit in midair after making a leaping catch.

San Francisco won its next two games, beating the Atlanta Falcons and Los Angeles Raiders. Against the Raiders, Rice caught 3 passes, for a total of 94 yards. He averaged more than 30 yards per catch in the game. The following week, however, problems began for both Rice and the 49ers. They lost to the New Orleans Saints, a poor team. Part of the problem was that Joe Montana had five of his passes dropped by his receivers. Rice was one of the players with the butterfingers.

Rice came back strongly the next week against the Falcons, however. He scored his first touchdown in a regular-season game on a 25-yard pass from Montana. Rice held the ball high above his head as he crossed through the end zone with Atlanta defensive back Jerry Butler still hanging on to the tail of his jersey.

In the following weeks, however, Rice had more problems with dropping passes. He was puzzled; he had never before had trouble hanging on to things, whether they were bricks or footballs. Joe Montana suggested that Rice was "trying to make the big play every time he caught the ball. Something that's typically rookie, he tried running with the ball before he caught it."[4]

A few years later, Rice talked about the difficulties he had during his first year. He thought part of the problem was adjusting to the change from small college football to the more complex offenses in the NFL. "At Mississippi Valley State, I had the option of running any route I wanted, and I became accustomed to that freedom, so when I got here I was thinking about my routes and not concentrating on the ball."[5]

Maybe professional football was really going to be harder than Rice had imagined. However, he kept trying. Instead of sulking, he just worked harder. "It was very difficult for me," he said about what he went through his rookie season, "but I think overall, it made me into a better football player."[6]

Even with the hard work and support from teammates, Rice had a few more bad games. Playing against the Kansas City Chiefs in November, he dropped a pass while wearing gloves. He took the gloves off, but it did not make a difference. A few minutes later, he dropped a pass barehanded. He finally caught his first pass of the game in the fourth quarter; however, right after the catch, he fumbled the ball, and the Chiefs recovered it. Two weeks later, in a game against the Washington Redskins, Rice was unable to make even a single catch. It would be the last time in his career that he would be shut out.

With the next game, he started a string of games in which he would have at least one reception. This streak would last for well over ten years. Rice started the streak in a big way. In a Monday night game against the Los Angeles Rams, a national television audience was watching, and Rice responded. He ended up catching 10 passes in the game. Rice also had a couple of big plays in the second half. With the 49ers behind, 10–7, Montana heaved an off-balance throw downfield. Rice caught it 50 yards beyond the line of scrimmage. He then pulled away from Rams' safety Nolan Cromwell for a 66-yard touchdown. It put San Francisco in the lead, 13–10.

The Rams tied the game with a field goal, but then Rice struck again. He beat rookie defensive back Jerry Gray for a 52-yard reception. Rice was stopped two yards short of the goal line, but it did set up another 49er touchdown. Rice finished the game with 241 yards receiving. That broke a team record that had been set by Dave Parks in 1965. Unfortunately, the Rams came back with two touchdowns in the fourth quarter, to beat the 49ers. "Without a victory," Rice said after the game, "it doesn't mean that much."[7] Still, the game was a turning point for Rice. After having dropped ten passes in his first thirteen games, he caught ten passes, all in one game. The world was starting to see how good Jerry Rice really was.

The Rice family itself got the chance to see how good Jerry was in the next game. They drove down to the game in New Orleans, and Rice treated them to a couple of important fourth-quarter receptions.

The 49ers were trailing the New Orleans Saints, 19–17. They planned a running play, but Montana changed the play call as he called out signals at the line of scrimmage. Changing a play right before the ball is snapped is called an audible. A quarterback may decide to do this when he sees how the defense is lined up. In this case, Montana decided he would rather try for a big play with Rice than try a running play.

Rice took off straight down the field, zooming past defender Johnnie Poe. Montana hit him with a beautiful pass, for a 42-yard gain. The play set up a touchdown that put San Francisco ahead. The 49ers padded their lead when they got the ball back on their next drive. They faced fourth down and decided not to go for a field goal; instead they would try for the first down. Montana fired a pass to tight end Russ Francis, but cornerback Willie Tullis knocked it out of his hands. Instead of falling to the ground for an incomplete pass, the ball popped into the air. Rice caught it on the fly and turned it into a big gain. That play set up another San Francisco touchdown. The 49ers won the game, 31–19. One game was left in the regular season, and the 49ers still were not assured of making the playoffs. The 49ers could not win the Western Division title; however, they could get a wild-card spot if they could win their final game.

They fell behind to the Dallas Cowboys, 13–0, but stormed back in the second half. Rice had another big game, catching 7 passes for 111 yards. He also scored a touchdown, but it was not on a pass. It came on a reverse late in the third quarter. Rice took a handoff from running back Derrick Harmon. He then shook off an arm tackle by blitzing Dallas linebacker Jesse Penn and outraced defensive end Jim Jeffcoat to the corner. Rice turned upfield and ran fifteen yards into the end zone.

Several times during the season, the 49ers had tried springing Rice loose on a reverse. Usually, it did not work very well. His first five reverse attempts averaged barely over two yards each. On the reverse for the touchdown against Dallas, Rice had to do it himself; films later showed that the 49ers had missed three blocks on the play. Teams that had questioned his speed were now seeing that he could turn on the burners.

The win against the Cowboys put San Francisco into the playoffs. However, the 49ers did not last long as they lost, 17–3, to the New York Giants. After winning the Super Bowl for the 1984 season, San Francisco was knocked out of the playoffs in the

Jerry Rice tries to maneuver his body to break away from a Dallas defender. In the final game of the 1985 season, Rice caught 7 passes for 111 yards as the 49ers defeated the Cowboys and gained a playoff berth.

opening round in 1985, but the players knew they would have more great years ahead of them. Rice knew he also had a bright future. He had a rocky beginning but a strong finish to the season. United Press International and the NFL Players' Association both picked Rice as the Rookie of the Year in the NFC.

Chapter 5

Making the Grade

The NFL offenses were more complex for Rice than what he had been used to in college, but he would have to adapt to that. Between the 1985 and 1986 seasons, Rice spent a lot of time reading the 49ers' playbook. It was a thick book, loaded with different types of plays, and Rice studied it until he had mastered it. Now the plays and the pass routes would be second nature to him. Instead of thinking about what he was supposed to be doing, he could just do it. This would leave his mind free to concentrate on things like catching the ball.

With an off-season of study behind him, Rice reported to training camp in 1986 loaded with confidence once again. The studying paid off. Rice would have an outstanding year, one that would amaze even Bill Walsh, who had never lost confidence in Rice. Walsh had figured it would take a few years for Rice to develop and become a star. During the 1986 season, however, Walsh changed his thinking. Rice was about two years ahead of the schedule Walsh had imagined for him.[1]

For Rice, a key game came against the Indianapolis Colts in the fifth week of the season. He had 6 catches for 172 yards. His catches included 3 touchdown receptions. Two of those were for more than forty yards each. "There was something about that game that put me on the right track," Rice later said. "I felt like I could do anything I wanted."[2]

The 1986 season was turning into a breakout year for him. What was really amazing was that Rice was doing this without having the best quarterback in the game to throw to him for half the season. Joe Montana ruptured a disk in his lower back in the first game of the season. It was a serious injury that required surgery a week later. Everyone thought he would miss the rest of the season, and some wondered if Montana would ever return. As it turned out, Montana came back just eight weeks later.

Backup quarterback Jeff Kemp filled in while Montana was gone. Rice and Kemp did well together.

Rice's big game against the Colts came with Kemp doing the passing. A few weeks later, Kemp got hurt and another quarterback, Mike Moroski, stepped in. The switch did not affect Rice. He kept rolling.

Rice wrapped up the regular season in fine fashion. In the final game, he made a terrific touchdown catch against the Los Angeles Rams. After having his face mask grabbed by one defender, he got away and recovered his speed. He then leaped between two other Rams to grab a pass that he turned into a 44-yard touchdown. Quarterback coach Mike Holmgren later said that the pass should not even have been thrown to Rice because he was so well covered. "It was an unbelievable effort," said Holmgren. "I still don't know how he did it."[3]

This was the first of thirteen straight regular-season games in which Rice would catch a touchdown pass. It would be a new NFL record. Rice ended the 1986 season with 86 catches, the most in the NFC. He led the entire NFL with 1,570 receiving yards, the third highest total in league history. He was voted to play in the Pro Bowl (the NFL's all-star game) and was named NFL Player of the Year by *Sports Illustrated* magazine.

All of the teams that had passed on Jerry Rice in

the draft were probably sorry that they had. Many did not think he was fast enough to be a great receiver in the NFL. Perhaps they had good reason for feeling that way. Rice's time for running the 40-yard dash was not that good. A good time is considered to be 4.4 seconds. Rice's time was usually 4.6 seconds. No one could really account for Rice's "game speed," however. Teammate Ronnie Lott said of Rice, "He may run a 4.6 for the clock, but when the ball is out there, he runs a 4.4."[4]

The 49ers won the NFL Western Division title and advanced to the playoffs. Once again, San Francisco's opponent would be the New York Giants. The game was scoreless in the first quarter, when Montana hit Rice with a pass. Rice had clear sailing ahead. No one stood between him and the end zone. But instead of an easy touchdown, the play became a disaster. The ball squirted loose from his hands even though no one was near him. As it turned out, the mistake did not make much difference in the outcome of the game. The Giants demolished the 49ers, 49–3. Even if Rice had scored a touchdown on the play, it would not have made much difference, but the fumble haunted him for some time. "That play will always linger in the back of my mind," he said a year later.[5]

The 1987 season may be best remembered for a

month-long strike by the NFL Players Association. Because of it, the NFL canceled one week of games altogether. The league then brought in replacement players to fill in until the strike was settled three weeks later.

Due to the strike, Rice played in only twelve regular-season games instead of the normal sixteen games. Even so, he set a new NFL record with 22 touchdown catches. When the strike was settled and the regulars returned, some players had trouble getting back in stride. Not Rice. He picked up where he had left off, scoring touchdowns as if he had never been gone.

At a game at Green Bay in early December, Rice caught a touchdown pass in his tenth regular-season game in a row. It was a beauty. The 49ers were clinging to a small lead in the fourth quarter when Rice took off on a slant pattern. Since Rice was covered by two Packers, Joe Montana kept his pass low so it would not be intercepted. It was a difficult pass to catch under any circumstances; being double-covered made it all the harder. But Rice caught the ball anyway. He then turned on his game speed and made it past two other defenders for a 57-yard touchdown that broke the game open. Years later, Rice still considered this catch to be among the best he ever made.

FACT

Jerry Rice does not mind being considered "flashy." As a result, he received the nickname "Flash 80" (the 80 referring to his uniform number). He even taped the words "Flash 80" to the bottom of his shoes, saying it gave him energy.

Being double-covered (and sometimes triple-covered) was becoming a way of life for Rice. He did not like it, but he accepted it. "Oh, I hate that," he once said about being double-teamed. "I guess I worked myself into this predicament." Someday, I would like to go out and just be like every receiver, one-on-one against a defensive back, and have some fun. . . ."[6]

Indeed, Rice had worked himself into that predicament. It was because he was so good that few defensive backs could contain him on their own. Rice knew, however, that double coverage on him meant fewer defenders would be covering the other San Francisco receivers. Jerry Rice was also extremely valuable, even when the ball was not thrown to him. He would still attract a crowd of defenders, and he often helped the 49ers in that way.

On December 14, the 49ers beat the Chicago Bears, 41–0. In the first quarter, Montana suffered a pulled hamstring and had to leave the game. Steve Young stepped in and fired 3 touchdown passes to Rice. Rice now had 18 touchdown catches for the season; tying the NFL record set by Mark Clayton of the Miami Dolphins in 1984. Rice broke Clayton's record in the next game, against the

Atlanta Falcons. Early in the third quarter, he caught a 20-yard touchdown pass from Young.

In addition to breaking Clayton's record for most touchdown catches in a season, Rice set another record on the play. It gave him a touchdown reception in his twelfth straight game. Elroy "Crazy Legs" Hirsch of the Los Angeles Rams had set a record with eleven straight games with a touchdown catch in 1950. Hirsch's record was tied by Buddy Dial of the Pittsburgh Steelers in 1959. The record would stand for another twenty-eight years before Rice broke it in 1987.

Jerry Rice's boyhood hero, Lynn Swann, was now admiring Rice. "Anybody can make one big catch for a touchdown," said Swann, "but to do it game after game is remarkable. For a receiver to have that kind of consistency is remarkable."[7]

Rice had another touchdown catch against the Falcons and finished the regular season with two more touchdowns against the Los Angeles Rams. The 49ers record of 13 wins and 2 losses was the best in the entire league. Rice received the National Football League's Most Valuable Player (MVP) award. He was the first 49er to be named MVP since quarterback John Brodie won the award in 1970.

It was a magical season for Rice and the 49ers. Unfortunately, it did not have a happy ending. They

Anthony Carter of the Minnesota Vikings eludes the pursuit of the San Francisco defense. It was Carter, not Rice, who had a big receiving game in the 1987 playoff series.

were heavy favorites in their first playoff game, against the Minnesota Vikings. But the Vikings shocked the 49ers, beating them, 36–24. Montana and Rice were both sluggish and could never get their game in gear. Rice finished with only 3 catches for only 28 yards. It was a disappointing way to end an otherwise great season, but Rice knew there would be more chances in the future.

Chapter 6

Super Seasons

The 49ers were determined to do better in postseason play in 1988, but first they would have to make the playoffs. Through much of the season, it was not a sure thing that this would happen. It took a while for the 49ers to display the form that San Francisco fans expected from them. For one thing, no one knew from one week to the next who the starting quarterback would be. Joe Montana and Steve Young battled for the job for the first half of the season. Coach Walsh finally decided that Joe Montana would be the team's starting quarterback. With that uncertainty out of the way, the 49ers won four of their last five games to win the NFC West divisional title for the third straight season.

The 49ers also had to overcome an injury to their

best receiver. Rice injured his ankle in a game against the Los Angeles Rams in mid-October and was bothered by it for several more weeks. He finished the year with just 64 receptions. However, he still had over thirteen hundred yards in receiving, thanks to some big catches along the way.

One of those catches came in the second game of the season, against the New York Giants. Young had started the game but was replaced by Montana in the second half. The 49ers trailed by four points with less than a minute left in the game and the ball at their own 22-yard line. Montana did not have any brainstorms to help him decide what to do next. Instead, a play was called that would be familiar to any kid who ever played football in a schoolyard in America—a Hail Mary. Everyone would go deep, and someone would try to get open.

Two of the San Francisco receivers ran straight down the middle of the field. They tied up the New York safeties, which left Giants' cornerback Mark Collins alone to try and stop Rice. Collins could not do it. Rice got a step on Collins, caught Montana's pass 33 yards downfield, and cruised another 45 yards into the end zone. The 78-yard touchdown gave the 49ers a 20–17 win. This was not Rice's longest touchdown of the season, though. That came at San Diego in late November. Rice caught a

96-yard touchdown pass from Montana to open the scoring in a game that the 49ers went on to win, 48–10.

After the strong finish in the regular season, the 49ers prepared for the playoffs. Their first opponent was Minnesota, the team that had eliminated them the season before. The Vikings had a lot of great players, but the 49ers were a great team. This time, there were no surprises. San Francisco demolished the Vikings, 34–9, as Rice caught 3 touchdown passes.

In the NFC championship game, San Francisco dominated again, beating the Chicago Bears, 28–3. Rice had another big game as he caught 2 touchdown passes, one of them for 61 yards. The win put the 49ers back in the Super Bowl for the first time in four years and the first time since Rice had joined them.

Their opponent would be the American Football Conference champions, the Cincinnati Bengals. A lot of Super Bowls end up with one team losing by a large margin. This one was a classic, though. It went down to the game's final minute before being decided.

The 49ers moved the ball well and racked up yards, but they had trouble getting the ball in the end zone. So did Cincinnati. All either team could manage in the first two quarters was a field goal, and the game was tied, 3–3, at halftime.

There were more field goals in the third quarter, one for each team, to make the score 6–6. Following the 49er field goal, though, Cincinnati's Stanford Jennings returned the kickoff 93 yards for a touchdown. Late in the third quarter, the 49ers were behind, 13–6. San Francisco came back quickly, however, and Rice was a key part of it. On the first play of the drive, Montana hit Rice for a 31-yard gain. Rice now had over 100 yards receiving in the game, but he was not done yet.

The 49ers made it to the Bengal 14-yard line. Montana decided to look for Rice again. Rice took off upfield, got past defensive back Lewis Billups, and cut for the corner. "I knew immediately we had a touchdown if I could throw it right," Montana said after the game.[1]

Montana threw it right. It still was not an easy journey to the end zone for Rice. After catching the ball, he had to twist and turn to stay in bounds. While falling, he extended his right hand with the ball over the goal line before the rest of his body landed out of bounds. It was a great play that tied the game.

Cincinnati broke the tie with another field goal and held a 16–13 lead late in the game. San Francisco

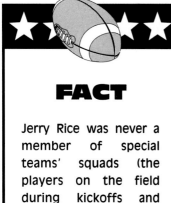

FACT

Jerry Rice was never a member of special teams' squads (the players on the field during kickoffs and punts). But early in his career he would sit in at special teams' meetings. He just wanted to be ready in case of an emergency.

Although he is double teamed, Jerry Rice leaps in the air to make another outstanding catch. Rice has often been able to out-jump the opposition and haul in a seemingly impossible reception.

got the ball back with just over three minutes to play. The 49ers were on their own 8-yard line, though, 92 yards away from the Cincinnati end zone. Fortunately, they had a quarterback who would not be fazed by what faced him. Montana went to work. He hit running back Roger Craig with an 8-yard pass, then connected with tight end John Frank for 7 more.

Rice then took a pass for a seven-yard gain, and the 49ers were moving. Three plays later, he caught a 17-yard pass, to move the ball into Cincinnati territory. Another pass to Craig put the ball at the Bengals' 35-yard line. Then trouble struck; the 49ers were penalized ten yards for having an ineligible receiver downfield. They needed a big play. Rice ran a slant pattern between three defensive backs, and Montana threw into the heavy coverage. If the ball had been intercepted, Montana would have been the one to blame, but Rice saved his quarterback. He outjumped the Bengal defenders and caught the ball at the 32, then ran for another 14 yards down to the 18-yard line.

Up to this point, the 49ers had just been hoping to get into field goal position so they could kick a field goal to tie the game and send it into overtime. Thanks to Rice's big play, though, they were now thinking touchdown. The winning score came two plays later, but it was not Rice's. It was because of Rice, however, that teammate John Taylor was able to get open in the end zone. Rice essentially was a decoy on the play. He went into motion as Montana called signals and turned upfield when the ball was snapped. Rice ran his pattern to the left of Taylor. Cincinnati safety Ray Horton was not sure which receiver he should follow. He hesitated too long, and Taylor was free. Taylor took the pass from Montana for the touchdown, and the 49ers were Super Bowl champions.

Rice did have plenty of catches in the game. His 11 receptions were good for 215 yards and his touchdown tied the game early in the fourth quarter. For his outstanding performance, Rice was voted the Super Bowl Most Valuable Player. His parents, who were at the game with the rest of the family, joined Rice on the podium as he accepted his award. It was a happy time for the 49ers. Four days later, however, the team received the news that they would have a new head coach for the next season. Bill Walsh announced that he would be stepping down as coach and moving into the San Francisco front office. Succeeding Walsh would be the team's long-time defensive coordinator, George Seifert.

The coach was different, but the results were the same for the 49ers in 1989. San Francisco was even

FACT

Jerry Rice was named the Most Valuable Player in the 49ers Super Bowl win over the Cincinnati Bengals even though he had sprained his ankle just a few days before. He had 11 catches in the game, including some important ones on San Francisco's game-winning drive. After the game, his coach, Bill Walsh, said, "Especially on that last drive, because of his sprained ankle, Jerry Rice was operating on nerve."[2]

better in the regular season than it had been the year before. The 49ers finished with a record of 14–2, best in the entire National Football League. Rice caught 82 passes and led the NFL with 1,483 receiving yards. Eight times during the year he had at least one hundred yards in a game. After having scored only 9 touchdowns in 1988, Rice rebounded and crossed the goal line 17 times in 1989.

The 49ers were finely tuned entering the playoffs and they did not let up. They whipped Minnesota in their playoff opener, as Rice had 2 touchdown catches, including one that covered 72 yards. San Francisco then had no trouble handling the Los Angeles Rams in the NFC championship game to earn a second straight appearance in the Super

The 49ers defeated the Cincinnati Bengals, 20–16, to become Super Bowl XXIII champions.

George Seifert (shown here) replaced the legendary Bill Walsh to become head coach of the San Francisco 49ers after the 1988 season.

Bowl. This time their opponents would be the Denver Broncos. It would be the fourth Super Bowl for each team. The difference between them was that the 49ers had never lost a Super Bowl game, and the Broncos had never won.

The trend continued. This Super Bowl was never in doubt, as San Francisco got off to an early lead and then kept increasing it. Rice opened the scoring with a 20-yard touchdown on the 49ers' first drive. He took Montana's pass at the 8-yard line, bounced off a defender, and found his way into the end zone.

Denver came back with a field goal, but the 49ers reeled off 5 straight touchdowns. Rice caught a 38-yard touchdown pass late in the second quarter and added another touchdown, this one covering 28 yards, early in the third quarter. He set a Super Bowl record with 3 touchdown catches as San Francisco won the game, 55–10.

The 49ers were on top of the football world. Some were calling them the team of the 1980s. Others went even further, saying that the 49ers were the best team ever. They were quick to add that the 49ers had the best receiver ever in Jerry Rice.

Chapter 7

Looking for More

Two Super Bowl rings were not enough to satisfy Jerry Rice. Like the rest of the 49ers, he wanted more. That constant hunger for victory was one of the things that made Rice and the 49ers great.

The 49ers got off to a good start in 1990, and so did Rice. The team had a 4–0 record as it went into a game against the Atlanta Falcons on October 14. The first time the 49ers got the ball, they drove down the field. On a play from the Atlanta 24-yard line, Rice took off downfield. Charles Dimry tried to give him a bump near the line of scrimmage but missed. It was his only chance of stopping Rice, who blew by him and took Montana's pass for an easy touchdown. Later in the quarter, the Falcons tried a blitz. A blitz involves a defense having one or more

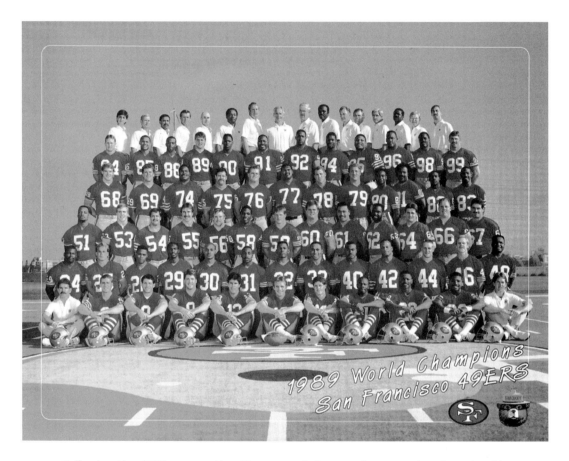

Following the 1989 season, the 49ers won their second consecutive championship when they defeated the Denver Broncos, 55-10, in Super Bowl XXIV. Rice is in the fourth row from the bottom, fourth from the right.

defensive backs rush the quarterback instead of laying back to help cover receivers. It can put pressure on a quarterback; however, if the quarterback can get his pass off quickly, he stands a good chance of finding an open receiver. In this case, the Atlanta blitz meant that Dimry was all alone in trying to stop Rice. The result was a 25-yard touchdown pass from Montana to Rice.

In the second quarter, Rice beat Dimry again and caught a 19-yard touchdown pass. Rice decided to pick on someone else in the second half. He scored on a 13-yard pass, as safety Scott Case was not able to cover him. In the final quarter, though, Rice went back to burning Dimry. He faked a move toward the goal post, then cut back to the sideline. Dimry bit on the fake and fell down trying to switch directions. Rice took a 15-yard pass into the end zone for his fifth touchdown catch of the game, to tie an NFL record. Rice caught 13 passes in the game, a San Francisco team record. His 225 yards for the day also put him past Dwight Clark as the 49ers' career leader in receiving yards.

The 49ers kept up their hot play into November. They beat the Dallas Cowboys, 24–6, to raise their season record to 9–0. Counting their playoff and Super Bowl wins from the previous season, it was the team's seventeenth straight win. Rice made some outstanding catches in the game. One was on San Francisco's first scoring drive. He made a catch good for a 37-yard gain as his head was being pulled back by the face mask by Dallas cornerback Issiac Holt. He made an even better grab on the team's next drive. It was not a long play, but it was spectacular as he leaped high to snag a 7-yard touchdown pass with one hand.

Other San Francisco players were used to seeing Rice make great catches. However, the two great receptions he made in the Dallas game left some of his teammates in a state of disbelief. "He is out of this world," said tight end Jamie "Spiderman" Williams. "Every week he just keeps coming up with plays that leave average human beings in awe."[1]

Rice went on to lead the National Football League with 100 receptions and 1,502 yards receiving. He was named Player of the Year by *Sports Illustrated*. The 49ers, after having won their first ten games of the year, finished the regular season with a 14–2 record, the best in the NFL.

The team seemed well on its way to another Super Bowl spot after easily beating the Washington Redskins in the first playoff game. The New York Giants were the next opponent in the NFC title game, however. The San Francisco defense was able to prevent the Giants' offensive line from scoring a touchdown. However, the New York defense was also tough.

The game was a battle of field goals until Montana hooked up on a long touchdown pass with John Taylor in the third quarter. That put the 49ers ahead, 13–6. New York came back with two more field goals by Matt Bahr but still trailed by a point late in the game.

The Giants had one last chance, following a Roger Craig fumble by the 49ers. The Giants drove downfield and scored on a 42-yard field goal. New York had a 15–13 win. The Giants, not the 49ers, would be going to the Super Bowl. It was a missed opportunity for the 49ers, and it would be several years before they would get back to the Super Bowl. Meanwhile, many things changed during that time.

The biggest change was at quarterback. Joe Montana had an elbow injury that caused him to miss the entire 1991 season. Steve Young, after many years as Montana's backup, was now the full-time quarterback. Young and Rice did not hit it off right away. They had problems communicating with one another. Rice also had to get used to catching passes from a left-handed quarterback. The ball spun in the opposite direction. It was not a big problem, but it was one more adjustment Rice had to make.

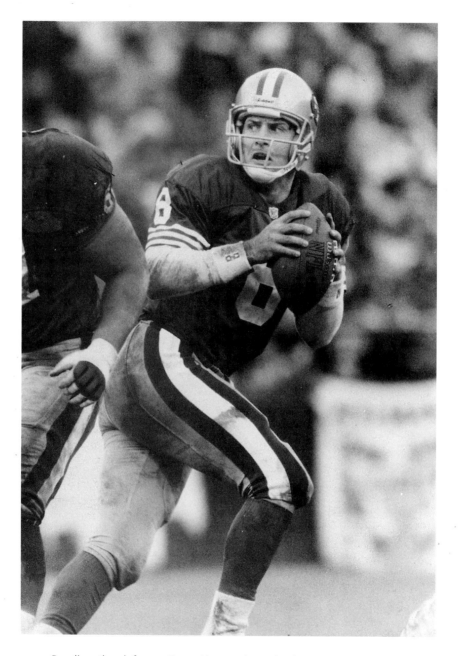

Reading the defense, Steve Young drops back to attempt a pass. After taking over for Joe Montana, Young became one of the best quarterbacks in the league.

"Steve is more of a running quarterback, so if the receivers are not open at the precise time, he's going to run with the ball," Rice said midway through the 1991 season. "Steve's game is to move around and make things happen, and he's not going to stand back there until the last second and dump the ball off. The second I might be getting open, Steve is going to be downfield running the ball. Joe on the other hand, would stand there in the pocket, and, if it takes that extra second to deliver the ball, he'll do it."[2]

Eventually Rice clicked with Young as well as, if not better than, he had with Montana. They took time to get going, however.

Even though Jerry Rice caught eight touchdown passes from Young in the first seven games of the season, the team was struggling. It won only three of those first seven games. Rice also hurt his knee early in the year. He suffered a slight tear in a ligament in his right knee, during a game against the Vikings. He kept playing, however, and did not even make the injury known to the public until the middle of November.

The slow start and an injury to Rice made it a difficult season for the 49ers. They did not even make the playoffs for the first time since Rice joined the team. They came back strongly in 1992, though.

FACT

It took Rice a little while to get used to Steve Young. However, he ended up catching more touchdowns in his career with Young than he had with Montana. Rice and Young also warmed up to one another and became very close. In fact, Rice refers to Young good-naturedly as "Uncle Steve."

FACT

Rice always looked up to Steve Largent, who held the record for career receiving touchdowns until Rice broke it. In fact, Rice chose Number 80 to wear because it was Largent's number. Largent was once on the cover of a Wheaties box. Rice keeps the box in his locker.

Mike Shanahan was the new offensive coordinator, and he maintained a game-day script sheet with a special list of plays designed to get the ball to Rice.[3]

Rice felt secure with the 49ers; he had signed a three-year contract extension with the team before the season started. He was also feeling more secure with Steve Young, who continued to be the 49ers' starting quarterback.

In a game against Atlanta on October 19, Rice scored 3 touchdowns, giving him more than one hundred for his career. Few players in the history of the NFL had ever reached that level. A few of those touchdowns had been runs, but 97 of them were pass receptions. He was closing in on Steve Largent's career record of 100 touchdown catches.

Rice tied the record in late November, in a game against Philadelphia. The record breaker came the next week against the Miami Dolphins. With a heavy rain falling throughout the game, the 49ers tried on several occasions to get a scoring pass to Rice. In the first half, he appeared to have the touchdown, but he stepped out of bounds just shy of the goal line. Finally, with ten minutes left in the game, the 49ers lined up with three receivers on the right side and one on the left. The receiver by himself on the left side was Rice. He ran a slant, took Young's pass

In November 1992, Jerry Rice broke Steve Largent's record by catching touchdown pass number 101.

in front of cornerback J. B. Brown, and kept running for a 12-yard touchdown and a new record.

The 49ers bounced back in 1992 to again post the best regular-season record in the NFL. Rice had 98 catches and led the NFL in receiving yards with 1,503. But their season ended in disappointment, as they lost to the Dallas Cowboys in the NFC title game. In 1993, it was more of the same. San Francisco faced the Cowboys for the NFC title. The Cowboys won again. Rice and the 49ers wondered if they would ever get back to the Super Bowl.

Chapter 8

A Matter of Style

"For me to play good [sic], I have to look good," says Jerry Rice. "My pants have to fit a certain way. My socks have to be pulled up to a certain length. That way, I feel like I'm ready to play."[1] Jerry Rice is always ready to play. He just feels better about it when he looks good—and looking good is important to Rice both at home *and* at work.

According to his wife, when Rice gets home after a game, he cleans house. He takes several showers a day and even spends time making sure that his socks are lined up in a particular order in his drawer. "Everything has to be in place," says Jackie. "His hair has to be perfect."[2] Jerry Rice's meticulous lifestyle matches his style of play on the field—precise, neat, and organized.

There is more, however, to being a great receiver than just being concerned with neatness. Whether he is taking a shower, washing his car, or polishing his helmet, Rice is also thinking about football. He is thinking about the 49ers next opponent, and the player who will be covering him. He is thinking about how he will get open so that he can catch long passes. He even thinks about things in his sleep.

"Every night before a game, I play the game in my mind while I'm in bed," Rice once said.

> My wife tells me all the time that I moan and groan in my sleep, that I may cuss or shake in bed. I don't mumble players' names. I put myself in a position to make plays. When I go into a ball game, it's almost like I know exactly what's going to happen because I played it the night before.[3]

This kind of visualization is common among top athletes. They play the game in their minds before stepping onto the field. They think about what is going to happen and what might happen. Then, when it does happen, they are ready.

Rice is ready because he does much more than think about football. The man is known for his tremendous work ethic. The day after one season ends—when most players go on vacation or take a rest—Rice begins preparing for the next season.

Through the summer months, he stays in shape, running many miles a day in sweltering heat. At times he has even run with a parachute attached to his back.

Jerry Rice runs up and down the many hills in San Francisco. One hill is particularly challenging. Regarding this hill, Rice says, "Mentally, you have to fight the quitting, and that transfers into making the big plays, the tough plays in the game. I put myself through this type of training, so I'm in the best shape of my life during the season."[4]

Rice's teammates admire him for his dedication and hard work. In 1994, quarterback Steve Young went to some members of the press and said:

> I want you to write about his [Rice's] work ethic because I want kids to understand that no matter how great you are, you don't get better unless you work hard. He's the greatest because of his work ethic.[5]

Rice drives himself to be the best. During the season, he checks the statistics of other top receivers in the league. "Sure, you look at the newspapers, you look at the stats," he says. "It helps motivate you to turn your intensity up a little more."[6]

In 1993 an article in a magazine suggested that Jerry Rice was only the third-best receiver in the NFL. The magazine said that Michael Irvin of the Dallas Cowboys and Sterling Sharpe of the Green Bay

Jerry Rice works just as hard in practice as he does in the games, which is why he has become perhaps the best receiver in football history.

Packers were better. Rice did not get upset. He just worked even harder to improve his game. He said that young stars like Irvin and Sharpe were prolonging his career. They were continuing to give him motivation to stay No. 1.

That motivation was there in 1994. The focus at the beginning of the season was more on Jerry Rice than on the San Francisco 49ers as a team. Fans across the country were watching to see when he would break Jim Brown's all-time record for touchdowns scored. San Francisco won its season opener as Rice broke Brown's record.

Even with the record out of the way, the 49ers lost two of their next four games. From then on, though, the team was nearly unstoppable. The 49ers won ten games in a row before finally losing to Minnesota in their final game of the regular season. By that time, they had already assured themselves of finishing with the best record in the NFL. As a result, Coach Seifert took Rice and Young out of the game early to make sure they did not suffer injuries with the playoffs coming up.

The Young-Rice tandem was awesome in 1994. Rice finished with 112 catches, his best performance ever. Young compiled one of the best seasons any quarterback had ever had and was named the NFL's Most Valuable Player.

A lot of people were pulling for Steve Young to do well. Although Young had been a part of two other San Francisco championship teams, he had spent more time on the bench than playing the game. During those years, Young was good enough to have started for many other NFL teams. The 49ers had Joe Montana as a starter, however. Young had to settle for being the team's backup quarterback.

Steve Young was now in his fourth year as the 49ers starting quarterback, but he had not yet been able to get the team to the Super Bowl. Jerry Rice was one of the people pulling for Young—and he was going to do whatever he could to help him.

San Francisco had no trouble beating the Chicago Bears, 44–15, in its playoff opener. To the 49ers, this was just a tuneup. Now they would play the Dallas Cowboys—the team that had ended their last two seasons—for the NFC title. The team that won this game would go to the Super Bowl. However, many people were calling this the real Super Bowl. After all, most fans figured that the 49ers and Cowboys were the two best teams in the entire league.

The 49ers were still stinging from their last two losses to Dallas in the NFC title game. This time, they came out storming and jumped to a quick lead. San Francisco scored three early touchdowns and led, 21–0. The Cowboys refused to quit, though. They battled back and trailed, 24–13, late in the first half. Now it was time for the 49ers to get tough again as they got the ball back with just over a minute before halftime.

The 49ers got down to the Dallas 28-yard line. Young then looked for the big play and went to Rice. Young connected with Rice in the back corner of the end zone for a touchdown that gave the 49ers a 31–13 lead. Young later called this the play of the game.[7] The 49ers went on to beat the Cowboys, 38–28. For the first time since the 1989 season, San Francisco was in the Super Bowl. Their opponent was the San Diego Chargers, a team playing in the Super Bowl for the first time. The 49ers were heavy favorites to beat the Chargers and wasted no time in getting going. Barely a minute into the game, Rice charged through the middle of the San Diego defense, got behind the safeties, and hauled in a long pass from Young that was good for a 44-yard touchdown.

Later in the first quarter, Rice ran a reverse and was smashed on his left shoulder by Darrien Gordon of the Chargers. He had to leave the game and go to the locker room to have his shoulder iced and taped. He had suffered a shoulder separation, and many wondered if he would return. Not only did Rice come back, he caught two more touchdown passes from Young in the second half. "Jerry Rice with one arm is better than anyone else with two arms," Steve Young said after the game.[8] The 49ers beat the Chargers, 49–26, to win the Super Bowl.

Rice had a great game. He caught 10 passes for 149 yards and scored 3 touchdowns. But the Most Valuable Player of the game was Steve Young, who set a Super Bowl record with 6 touchdown passes.

There were records galore broken in this game. Rice's three scores gave him 7 career Super Bowl touchdown catches, more than any other player. The 49ers also became the first team to ever win 5 Super Bowls (two of them before Rice joined the 49ers).

Records were on people's minds as the 1995 season opened. Rice was closing in on a couple of career receiving marks. One was the record for most receiving yards in a career, 14,004, held by James Lofton. The record for catches in a career was 934, held by Art Monk. Monk was still active in 1995, but he played very little and had few receptions during the year. Halfway through the season, Rice passed Lofton, but it did not look like he would be able to catch Monk before the season ended. Rice had some great games near the end of the year, however. He caught 14 passes against the Vikings in the second-to-last game, giving him 110 catches for

Jerry Rice became a member of his third championship team when the 49ers whipped the San Diego Chargers, 49–26, in Super Bowl XXIX. Rice is in the fourth row from the bottom, second from the right.

Art Monk is considered by many to be one of the best receivers to ever play professional football. During the 1995 season, Jerry Rice broke Monk's record for most passes caught in a career.

the year. Rice became the first player ever to have three seasons with at least 100 receptions.

In the 49ers final regular-season game, Rice had 12 receptions to finish with 122, his best-ever total. It was also enough to push him past Monk and become the career leader in pass receptions. Rice also had 1,848 receiving yards in 1995, an NFL single-season record. Rice kept the hot hand into the playoffs. However, the 49ers ran into an even hotter team in the Green Bay Packers. Green Bay upset San Francisco, 27–17, ending the 49ers season. For Jerry Rice, however, the end of one season meant preparing for the next. After all, he has a job to do— and it is this job that allows him to provide a nice lifestyle for his family. Jerry and Jackie Rice have three children: daughter Jaqui, born in 1987; son Jerry, Jr., born in 1991; and second daughter Jada, born in 1996. The Rice family also has four dogs, all Rottweilers.

There were more milestones for Jerry Rice in 1996. In a November game at New Orleans, Rice caught a nine-yard pass from Steve Young and was forced out of bounds just short of the goal line. It was the one thousandth reception of his career. He was the first player ever to reach that level. The following month, Rice caught his one hundredth pass of the season, making him the first receiver ever to catch at least 100 passes in three straight seasons. Rice finished the year with 108 receptions for 1,254 yards and 8 touchdowns, giving him 1,050 receptions, 16,337 receiving yards, and 154 touchdowns for his career. These were all records.

Jerry Rice does more than just set records, however. He is a team player who cares first about winning games. The 49ers had another good year in 1996, but, once again, they were eliminated from the playoffs earlier than they would have liked. They beat the Philadelphia Eagles in the first round, before being knocked out by the Green Bay Packers, the eventual Super Bowl champions.

Jerry Rice signed a contract extension at the end of the 1996 season. The opening game of the 1997 season brought adversity Rice's way, however. In a loss to the Tampa Bay Buccaneers, he injured his left knee when he was tackled in the second quarter. Rice, who had never missed a game in his career, had reconstructive knee surgery and returned to play in one more game only to suffer another knee injury which kept him out for the rest of the season.

Someday, Jerry Rice may look back on his career and bask in the knowledge that he was the best ever—but not yet. There is still more to be done. "I don't dwell on the past," Rice says. "There's always a new challenge. It's what I can do now that matters."[9]

Chapter Notes

Chapter 1

1. Ira Miller, "49ers Focus in a Class by Himself," *San Franscisco Chronicle*, November 22, 1990, p. D1.

2. Scott Ostler, "Flash 80," *Sport*, February 1994, p. 46.

3. Ibid.

4. Tom Fitzgerald, "The San Francisco Treat," *The Sporting News*, January 4, 1988, p. 12.

5. John Crumpacker, "49ers Romp in Rice Bowl," *San Francisco Examiner*, September 6, 1994, p. D1.

Chapter 2

1. Roy S. Johnson, "Rice Has 49ers in Good Hands," *The New York Times*, December 14, 1987, p. C1.

2. Ralph Wiley, "Rice Is a Breed Apart," *Sports Illustrated*, September 28, 1987, p. 41.

3. Tom Fitzgerald, "The San Francisco Treat" *The Sporting News*, January 4, 1988, p. 12.

4. Rick Telander, "Let's Hand It to Him," *Sports Illustrated*, December 26, 1994, p. 43.

5. Wiley, p. 41.

6. Ibid.

Chapter 3

1. Jaime Diaz, "He's the Catch of the Year" *Sports Illustrated*, November 14, 1983, p. 71.

2. Frank Cooney, "Rice Joins NFL Receiving Elite," *San Francisco Examiner*, November 29, 1992, p. C1.

3. Diaz, p. 71.

4. Ibid.

Chapter 4

1. Ira Miller, "Moore Surprises 49ers—Agrees to Contract," *San Francisco Chronicle*, July 24, 1985, p. 59.

2. Ibid.

3. Art Spander, "Rice Leaves His Mark on Hallowed Turf," *San Francisco Examiner*, December 7, 1992, p. C1.

4. *Current Biography Yearbook*, 1990, p. 526.

5. Roy S. Johnson, "Rice Has 49ers in Good Hands," *The New York Times*, December 14, 1987, p. C1.

6. Tom Fitzgerald, "Record Night for Rice," *San Francisco Chronicle*, December 10, 1985, p. 63.

7. Denise Tom, "Jerry Rice," *USA Today*, January 8, 1988, p. 10E.

Chapter 5

1. *Current Biography Yearbook*, 1990, p. 526.

2. Ibid.

3. Tom FitzGerald, "The San Francisco Treat," *The Sporting News*, January 4, 1988, p. 12.

4. Paul Attner, "Reception Committee," *The Sporting News*, December 15, 1986, p. 12.

5. Pete Axthelm, "The 49er with the Golden Hands," *Newsweek*, January 11, 1988, p. 62.

6. Ira Miller, "49ers Focus in a Class by Himself," *San Francisco Chronicle*, November 22, 1990, p. D1.

7. Tom Fitzgerald, "The San Francisco Treat," *The Sporting News*, January 4, 1988, p. 12.

Chapter 6

1. Tom Dienhart, Joe Hoppel, Dave Sloan, eds., *The Sporting News Complete Super Bowl Book* (St. Louis, Mo.: The Sporting News Publishing Co., 1992), p. 281.

2. Ralph Wiley, "Rice Is a Breed Apart," *Sports Illustrated*, September 28, 1987, p. 43.

Chapter 7

1. Frank Cooney, "Flash! Rice Saves the 49ers," *San Francisco Examiner*, November 12, 1980, p. D1.

2. Ira Miller, "Rice: History Is in His Hands," *San Francisco Chronicle*, November 9, 1992, p. C8.

3. Ibid.

Chapter 8

1. Denise Tom, "Jerry Rice," *USA Today*, January 8, 1988, p. 10E.

2. Ibid.

3. "Night Moves," *People*, September 26, 1994, p. 112.

4. Dan Dieffenbach, "Preparing Rice," *Sport*, July 1995, p. 22.

5. John Crumpacker, "Simply the Best," *San Francisco Examiner*, September 4, 1994, p. C1.

6. Scott Ostler, "Flash 80," *Sport*, February 1994, p. 48.

7. *Sports California*, Spring 1995, p. 6.

8. Art Spander, "Rice: Battered by Triumphant," *San Francisco Examiner*, January 30, 1995, p. S3.

9. Art Spander, "Even Rice Can't Outrun March of Time," *San Francisco Examiner*, August 29, 1991, p. D5.

Career Statistics

Year	Team	G	REC	YDS	YPC	TDS
1985	San Francisco 49ers	16	49	927	18.9	3
1986	San Francisco 49ers	16	86	1,570	18.3	15
1987	San Francisco 49ers	12	65	1,078	16.6	22
1988	San Francisco 49ers	16	64	1,306	20.4	9
1989	San Francisco 49ers	16	82	1,483	18.1	17
1990	San Francisco 49ers	16	100	1,502	15.0	13
1991	San Francisco 49ers	16	80	1,206	15.1	14
1992	San Francisco 49ers	16	84	1,201	14.3	10
1993	San Francisco 49ers	16	98	1,503	15.3	15
1994	San Francisco 49ers	16	112	1,499	13.4	13
1995	San Francisco 49ers	16	122	1,848	15.1	15
1996	San Francisco 49ers	12	108	1,254	11.6	8
1997	San Francisco 49ers	2	7	78	11.1	1
Totals		186	1,057	16,455	15.6	155

G—Games
REC—Receptions
YDS—Yards
YPC—Yards per catch
TDS—Touchdowns

Where to Write
Jerry Rice

Mr. Jerry Rice
c/o San Francisco 49ers
4949 Centennial Boulevard
Santa Clara, CA 95054

On the Internet at:
http://www.nfl.com/players/profile/2772.html

Index

Southern Mississippi at
Hattiesburg,
University of, 28
Southern University, 28, 30,
31, 32
Swann, Lynn, 16–17, 57

T

Taylor, John, 67, 75
Texas Southern University,
28
Totten, Willie (Satellite),
26–27, 28, 30
Tullis, Willie, 46

V

Vanderbilt University, 33

W

Walsh, Bill, 31, 35, 36, 38, 52,
61, 67
Walters, Danny, 41
Washburn University, 30
Washington Redskins, 44, 74
Washington, Lionel, 12
Watters, Ricky, 12

Y

Young, Steve, 11, 12, 14, 56,
57, 61, 75, 77, 83, 85,
86–88

About the Author

Stew Thornley is an award-winning author and researcher who has written numerous sports books for young readers and adults. He has also co-authored a children's science book with his wife, Brenda Himrich. Stew and Brenda enjoy spending time with their cat, Poncé.